CRIMINAL
BEHAVIOUR

CRIMINAL
BEHAVIOUR

The Funniest and Most Explicit

Stories from Law Enforcement

Compiled by Robbie Guillory

**FREIGHT
BOOKS**

First published October 2014

Freight Books
49-53 Virginia Street
Glasgow, G1 1TS
www.freightbooks.co.uk

A CIP catalogue reference for this book is available
from the British Library

ISBN 978-1-908754-70-7
eISBN 978-1-908754-71-4

Printed and bound by Bell and Bain, Glasgow

Cover Illustration: Heather Brennan

Introduction

Working in the criminal justice system can be grim. One sees the worst side of life. Daily examples of just how angry, selfish, violent, generally malevolent and malicious ordinary folk can be.

Many of us, the great British public, are damaged, by our upbringing or life's experiences, in ways that make our behaviour self-destructive, downright dangerous or just plain criminal. For those tasked with protecting us from ourselves, it can feel like a war...

But from time to time things happen that lighten the mood, demonstrating that there's 'nowt as strange as folk...'

Our gallant law enforcement officers, probation and security professionals, lawyers and border force personnel, catch regular sight of the humanity of those they deal with, day in and day out, in often hilarious scenarios.

Invariably it's gross stupidity on show, sometimes perversion or just jaw-dropping brass neck. Sometimes circumstances conspire against the individual in tragic but comical fashion.

After many months of research, talking to police officers of all ranks, lawyers and others, I've compiled a collection of the best stories of those who've been at the front-line of law enforcement.

Some will make you laugh, some might even make you might cry, or wince in imagined pain, others may stretch credulity. But each has been told to me personally and in confidence and I've no reason to doubt their veracity. The law being what it is, all contributors' identities have been protected and, in some cases, details amended to protect the guilty and innocent.

I owe a great debt of thanks to all those busy professionals who took time, and a degree of personal risk, to share their tales.

Robbie Guillory

The Devil Finds Work

I was driving a police minibus, transporting 15 fellow officers to a mid-week premier league football match where we were all on duty. It was a gloomy winter's day and almost dark although it was only about 4pm. We were stuck in a motorway traffic jam and I was getting worried that we'd miss the briefing.

We were in the middle lane surrounded by gridlocked traffic. As I prepared to move into the outer lane I looked across at the hatchback alongside us just as the interior light was switched on. The young man driving was being vigorously fellated by a young woman.

He must have sensed he was being watched. His expression when he met the gaze of 16 serving police officers was unforgettable. And, yes, driver and passenger were both arrested and charged.

Constable, Manchester

Not by the hair on my chinny-chin-chin

We were called out to an armed robbery at a local corner shop. Unusually, the crime had been committed by a woman brandishing a screwdriver. Some cash, alcohol and cigarettes had been taken. The elderly proprietor gave us a detailed description.

Tall, long blond hair, attractive and wearing a summer dress with a floral pattern and a small pink cardigan. Not the usual attire for a criminal. The owner repeated several times that the woman was 'attractive'. He was clearly smitten. I believed there was still the chance of catching her on the street so I and my colleague called it in and then jumped in our car and drove around the area. Soon enough we spotted her walking ahead of us.

The description was spot on and she was carrying an opened bottle of vodka in her hand. We pulled up alongside, jumped out and arrested the woman on the spot. However, the shopkeeper was inaccurate in one key respect.

'She' was a male transvestite with thick black stubble.

Constable, London

A Little Tied Up

Working in CID, there was one particularly unpleasant felon on our manor that we'd been chasing for several years.

We suspected he had a friend on the force because whenever we tried to arrest him he had a habit of escaping our clutches at the last minute, earning the nickname 'the Hoxton Houdini'. His luck ran out when we received a tip-off from a woman who refused to leave her name, claiming he was "holed-up" in a house around half a mile from the station.

We responded immediately, stationing officers at the front and back of the property in case he tried to leg it. We needn't have bothered. When we broke down the door we found him upstairs, face down, arms and legs handcuffed to the bedframe, with a vibrator in his rectum. It was still running. Holed-up indeed.

Detective Sergeant, London

Silly Goat

I had the dubious pleasure of arresting a guy caught having sex with a goat. He'd been committing the offence in a field of tall grass to conceal the act from passers-by.

However, he didn't realise the field was next to a main railway line. As he was undertaking this hidious act of bestiality with his trousers round his ankles the 10.40 express to London Kings Cross came to a halt at a signal stop next to the field. At that moment 300 witnesses turned to see him doing what he was doing.

What was worst about the incident was that, on arresting him, no word of a lie, the perpetrator uttered the immortal words, 'But she was asking for it.'

Constable, Bedford

One Track Mind

One of the more unusual incidents I've had to deal with in my career was on a train only a couple of years ago. One night I had been arresting a verbally abusive fair dodger and was travelling back on the return service when I was asked to help the guard with a young woman locked in a toilet.

The door appeared unlocked and there was some movement but there was a large and heavy object against it trapping her inside. The passenger was becoming increasingly distressed but sounded worse for wear and wasn't making much sense.

We tried to force the door but she became hysterical and we worked out she wasn't alone. Her companion, a man, was slumped unconscious against the door. Together the guard and I used our combined strength to prise the door open slowly and carefully so as not to injure the guy. This took some time and when we did eventually get the door open we were met with a horrific scene.

There was blood all over the walls of the toilet. The woman was covered in blood. The unconscious man was naked and covered in blood. I immediately feared the worst, that there'd been a brutal crime of passion. But checking the man, he was alive, breathing and his pulse was normal. I couldn't see any obvious wounds. I called for an ambulance to meet us at the next station and tried get an idea of what had happened, while the other passengers in the carriage ear-wigged furiously.

It transpired that the couple were returning from a boozy night out. Inflamed by alcohol they'd decided to have sex in the toilet. Inside, he'd stripped off and they'd been hard at it over the toilet bowl when, probably due to the state his girlfriend was in, he'd ripped his foreskin badly. Blood had squirted everywhere and he'd fainted at the sight, hitting his head on the way down. The moral? Wait till you get home.

WPC, Glasgow

Short Sharp Shock

Early in my career I was one of the local constables covering a large estate.

Amongst the under-employed youth of the area there was a craze for collecting car badges. The better the car the more desirable the badge. A local businessman, who we knew was involved in what I'll call the 'pharmaceuticals' industry, was getting increasingly pissed off that the kids kept nicking the badges off a top-of-the-range BMW that sat gleaming in his driveway.

Being the uncompromising character that he was, he decided to take matters into his own hands. We found out about this when we were called to the scene of an incident. A fifteen year old had been thrown ten feet onto said businessman's lawn where he was lying slowly smoking, his tracksuit top blackened up one side.

The BMW owner thought he'd electrify the bonnet (and fifth replacement badge) on his car, in the way a farmer would electrify a fence.

Rather than connecting it to a car battery, though, which would deliver a small, unpleasant shock, he connected directly to the mains. Bang.

Detective Inspector, Liverpool

Banged to Rights

I worked in Vice for a few years, a singularly depressing job without much relief, if you pardon the pun. However, those who think that working girls are vulnerable victims might be well served by this story. Over the course of six months, many of the girls we came across complained of one particular punter who had a habit of sampling the merchandise then refusing to pay. Fairly common in the sex industry, but this guy was a habitual offender. He NEVER paid. He'd disguise himself so as not to be rumbled and would never visit the same girl twice. The workers, however, were determined to get even.

Eventually his past caught up with him. He'd booked two girls for a threesome in a hotel room at the airport. After buying them some drinks in the bar, they'd gone upstairs. As they got down to brass tacks, they'd somehow sussed who he was and when he was at his most vulnerable, they struck. An hour later we were called by hotel security. When we arrived we found a naked, middle-aged man in a hotel room screaming the place down, his foreskin nailed to the dressing table.

Detective Chief Inspector, Manchester

Love Thy Neighbour

As we all know, disputes between neighbours can get out of hand. Something about the proximity of the combatants makes all reason go out of the window.

The most extreme I experienced first-hand was between two well-off, middle-aged, middle-class guys who were having a boundary dispute. It seemed clear, on the many occasions we were called out, that the older one, in his sixties, was a nasty piece of work, who was picking a fight for the sake of it.

He would intimidate the other guy's wife a lot, standing in front of her car when she was trying to park, yelling and balling, slashing their car tyres at night, and even going to the length of, allegedly, poisoning the family dog. The worst thing for us was that the nutter was an ex-copper. The death of the dog seemed to be the last straw for the younger man. It turned out he'd made his money through cavity wall insulation.

One day, when the retired cop was out, the guy drove one of his trucks up and passed a hose through an open window.

Basically, he filled the guy's house full of cavity insulation foam. Almost every room. I was called to the trial and the damage was estimated at tens of thousands. Insulation man was given a custodial sentence but I've never seen a bigger grin on someone's face when they were led from the dock.

Sergeant, Worcester

May Contain Nuts

We once caught a guy who'd broken into a food processing plant. He jemmied a fire door in the belief that it wasn't alarmed or that he'd be in and out quick enough not to get collared. He was though, by me.

Partly because it was alarmed, but mainly because he'd swelled up to twice his normal size and was minutes from death. Although he knew he had an allergy, he didn't realise he was breaking into a peanut factory.

Constable, Rotherham

Your Sex is on Fire

Alcohol is usually the key ingredient in house fires, but not always how you imagine. Together with the Fire Brigade, we were called to a blaze in a small terrace in a nice area.

A young professional guy's wife was away and he had a few mates round. They got pissed up, then someone dared someone else to pour brandy over his penis and set it on fire. One then another had done this successfully, to great hilarity. Then one particularly hairy individual tried it, egged on by his drunken pals. Not only did he set fire to the brandy, he also ignited his pubes and chest hair. In the commotion he set fire to the curtains and the rest of the living room. One trip to A&E and another to IKEA.

Constable, Cardiff

Tight arse

I arrested a jewel thief once. In a posh arcade shop, he'd asked to look at a very expensive ring and, having distracted the assistant, proceeded to try and place the five figure diamond inside his rectum. While he'd gone to the extent of wearing jogging trousers and no pants for easy and quick access, he hadn't prepared sufficiently. Having forgotten to lubricate, and in the adrenalin rush of the heist, he'd been over-enthusiastic in his 'ramming' and had badly ripped the sensitive skin around that part of his anatomy on the gem's sharp gold mounting.

There was blood everywhere. He said that he'd just wanted to get his girlfriend something nice.(And stick it up his...).

Detective Inspector, Cheltenham

Bind Us Together, Lord

I stopped a vicar who was driving erratically. He was in the full outfit, linen suit, dog collar, the works.

He seemed pleasant enough. But then we heard a noise from the boot. We asked him to open up and behold, two balding sixty year old men were tied up naked, with gimp gags in their mouths. Takes all sorts.

Turned out it was totally consensual and nobody was making a complaint. All we could do was warn him about carrying passengers in an inappropriate manner.

Sergeant, York

Ding Dong

I was called to a house after a complaint by a woman about her neighbours. They'd be undertaking some garden topiary, which included a bush in the shape of a phallus.

It had been 'erected' two weeks before, and the woman next door was apoplectic with rage. I interviewed the couple.

They said they thought it would be funny. It was.

Constable, Scarborough

Great Escape

I arrived at the scene of a knife attack
in the town centre, prepared to have
to use physical force. However, the
perpetrator was the one on the ground,
bleeding profusely from the leg.

It turned out that when he'd tried to
intimidate his victim, he tripped over a
bit of pavement and stabbed himself in
the thigh. Not life threatening but things
got worse at A&E. He tried to make a run
for it in his hospital gown, spotty bare
backside visible to all.

WPC, Chesterfield

Total Arson

I was called about investigating a burglar alarm activation at a school. I decided to walk the perimeter with my dog, Bodie. He's a brilliant search dog and led me to a window panel that was held in place by gaffer tape. We entered, and, following procedure, I announced that I was about to release my dog. Receiving no response, I unleashed Bodie who immediately shot off down the corridor. I heard his claws rattling on the stairs, then an excited yelp, followed by a low growl. Quickly after, a shout of pain.

I ran upstairs and found him in a first floor classroom where he was gripping the leg of a young guy who'd dropped a large box of matches and a can of petrol. As I was calling it in, he said, "I'm sorry officer, you are quite right, I intended to burn the school down. By the way... do you think that this will influence my application to join the Police?"

Sergeant, London

One Born Every Minute

A small hotel in the centre of town requested police assistance with an unruly and potentially dangerous guest who'd just put a TV through his bedroom window.

When I arrived, I could easily see the culprit's room on the second floor with a smashed telly lying in the car park below.

As soon I saw him at the front desk, I could see the man in question was just a normal bloke, not someone I'd expect to be reprimanding for such a rock and roll act of destruction, although in this job you learn appearances can be deceptive.

However, with great embarrassment, he explained that he had been in his room when he got a call from someone claiming to be the receptionist.

They told him there was a gas leak and that he had to ventilate in his room by any means - urgently. We never caught the hoaxer but I'm certain it was an inside job.

Constable, Brighton

Too Much Information

Planning to rob a bank? Pay attention to what you write your demands on.

I caught the guy who, when he handed over a note to the teller asking for all her money, didn't realise is that he'd written it down on the back of his pay slip. Muppet.

Detective Sergeant, London

Pimp My Ride

I had been working an armed robbery case, and gave one of the witnesses my work phone number, just in case she had any more information.

A few months later I received a strange text message from an unknown number. It was in a kind of text speak I could barely decipher, so I replied saying that she had the wrong number. She responded saying, in forthright language, that she had a shed-load of drunks looking for sex and was I interested in getting in on the action? I met her in a car park with some back-up and charged her with soliciting.

Detective Sergeant, Birmingham

Drink Responsibly

Late one night, I spotted a car on the side of the road, passenger door open, interior light on.

Thinking someone had broken down, I stopped in front and got out of the car to see if they needed help. I found a man slumped over his steering wheel with a can of Tennent's Super upended on his lap and a kebab in his hand. I rapped on the driver's window until he woke up. He took one look at uniform, gunned the engine and shot forward, straight into the back of my police car.

Sergeant, Edinburgh

Planting Evidence

I was out one morning for a run in the local park, when I spotted several small Tupperware boxes tucked under a bush.

My professional curiosity kicked in. Inside each there were what looked very like individual packages of cannabis, each diligently wrapped in cling film. There must've been several thousands' worth there, so I called for assistance. When two on-duty colleagues arrived, they got excited too. A major find. Until a passing parky explained they were boxes of baby conifers due for planting the next day.

Sergeant, Inverness

Love Drunk

A woman appeared at the station desk one night demanding to be given a breathalyzer to prove to her embarrassed-looking girlfriend that she wasn't drunk.

I explained that we didn't do these on-demand, but she told me that she'd driven 10 miles expressly for this purpose after being accused by her partner. So I gave her the test and, of course, she failed. She was charged on a drink driving offence. But nice when the criminals come to you.

Sergeant, Cambridge

Crossing the Line

I was called to a house where someone had been stealing a woman's underwear from the clothes line. We always take these cases seriously in case it's a precursor to something more serious.

Both husband and wife were what can only be described as clinically obese and on several occasions the deviant had made off with some of woman's extremely large, racy lingerie. I advised them to keep their eyes peeled, and maybe invest in a security camera.

A couple of days later the wife called me to say they had witnessed a theft. I asked if she could give more as much info as possible. She gave a highly detailed description, covering the thief's hair, build, clothing and even his eye colour. I asked if they'd bought a high quality CCTV system. 'No,' she said. 'My husband's currently sitting on him.'

Detective Sergeant, Rhyl

Faulty Jeans

Shoplifting is one of those crimes that the police struggle with. It rarely leads to a conviction unless Security catch the thief in the act.

I remember an instance when a shoplifter had slipped out of their old worn jeans and made off with an expensive designer pair worth well over £200. Helpfully, in the back pocket of the discarded pair she'd left her bank card. If that wasn't bad enough, 20 minutes later she came back to retrieve it. I was waiting.

Store Detective, Southampton

No Ball Games

I was approached in the middle of a busy shopping precinct by two women in a state of alarm who had just been asked a rather strange request by a young man. 'Would you mind kicking me in the balls?' he'd said with a leer.

Turns out they did mind, and so did a couple of other people who reported the same thing. It wasn't long before someone obliged him, and then, surprise, surprise, he wasn't very difficult to catch.

Store Detective, Wolverhampton

Don't Do It

I was on the beat when I saw a bloke in his twenties sitting on a windowsill, his legs dangling over the ledge. I did what any decent copper would do and assumed the worst, that he was going end it all as pavement pizza, maybe taking a passing pedestrian with him.

I tried to initiate a conversation in the most empathetic manner I could manage. But before he could hear what I had to say, the guy disappeared back inside, knocking something off the windowsill which smashed at my feet. An ashtray.

Constable, Colchester

Bare Arsed Cheek

I was called to a pub following a complaint about a man who kept dropping his trousers. Sure enough, when I arrived there was a drunken lout with his trousers round his ankles.

Seeing me, he pulled them up and ran out of the bar only to trip and fall when his joggies dropped around his feet again.

On apprehending him, he complained that it wasn't his fault, his trousers wouldn't stay up because of the amount of small change he had in his pockets. To which the landlord, who'd followed me outside, said, 'So you're the wee shit who broke into the fruit machine!'

WPC, Glasgow

See No Evil

These days, airport scanners are highly accurate, but in the old days the imaging wasn't quite so clear.

We'd just scanned a woman's bag and there was, what appeared to be, some kind of martial arts weapon in her hand luggage. We asked the passenger to empty her bag for us so we could identify, and most probably confiscate, the item.

The woman seemed flustered, reassuring us repeatedly that she wasn't carrying anything she shouldn't be. This only made us more suspicious. She finally agreed to empty the bag, giving us, and the passengers behind her, an eyeful of what I can only describe as the most disturbing sex aid I have ever seen. 'Special-interest' in today's parlance.

The lesson? If you don't want us to see it, put it in the hold!

Airport Security Officer, Heathrow

Pot Luck

One of the best lessons I've learned in this job is to always expect the worst.

When I went through training at Hendon, I don't know what I'd have said if I'd been warned that someday I'd pull a guy over for drunk driving, only to find him naked from the waist down with his penis in a pot of yoghurt.

Sergeant, Leeds

Write and Wrong

A young lad of eleven years had been caught shoplifting pencils, rubbers and other items of stationery from WH Smith.

The boy appeared at the Juvenile Court with his father. The father was invited into the witness box to give evidence on behalf of his son – to discuss his character. He opened his statement by saying 'I've told him time and time again, if he wants anything like what he took from the shop, I can get it for him from work!'

Solicitor, Oxford

A Study in Scarlet

I was giving a talk at a local primary school, and some parents had joined us. One of the braver seven year olds raised his hand and asked if he could have my handcuffs to take home.

I had to say, 'I'm afraid not, son. I need these for work.' He then said, 'That's okay, my mummy and daddy have a furry pair in their bedroom.' I could tell which one was his mother. The woman with the beetroot face.

Constable, Newcastle-upon-Tyne

No Laughing Matter

I was working in an inner city in the 1980s and had a particularly tough estate on my patch. I was called to one flat in a high-rise, around 16 flights up, after neighbours complained of incessant barking. I knocked on the door, and the tenant, an ordinary looking guy in his 40s, answered. I could see the dog in question standing behind him. However, it was no conventional pet. The conversation went something like this:

'Sir, are you Mr X, the tenant?'

'Yes, I am.'

'We've had a complaint about excessive noise coming from an animal being kept at this property. Is that the animal kept here?' [I point at the beast behind him].

'Er, yeah. S'ppose so.'

'Can I ask what kind of animal it is?'

'It's a dog, innit.'

'I don't think it is, sir.'

'Yeah, it is. It's an African Mountain Dog. Bloke said it was.'

'I'm sorry but I don't think it is, sir.'

'What d'you mean?'

'I'm no expert but I've watched enough David Attenborough to know that's a hyena. You do know that hyenas are dangerous wild animals, don't you?'

'He's not doing any harm. Don't take him away. The kids love him...'

Needless to say he was lucky to keep the flat. Beware of men in pubs selling 'puppies'.

Sergeant, Leeds

Behind Closed Doors

We caught a guy trying to steal a high performance car from a suburban house.

The couple had been woken in the night to the sound of the garage door creaking shut. The husband realised he'd left it unlocked, belted down the stairs, got the keys, ran outside and locked the thief in.

After that it was just a matter of calling us. When the first officers arrived he was baiting the bloke through the locked shutter, really letting rip, issuing some very unpleasant threats. As tempted as I'm sure he was, the thief resisted the urge to smash up the vehicle as it would've guaranteed a custodial sentence. The guy had some self-control, unlike the owner.

Detective Inspector, Cheshire

Shit the Missus Says

I was working late on a Friday night, close to Christmas, when a man was brought in for drink driving. I normally don't even look up when these guys come in.

However, as he confiscated the bloke's property, including his mobile, the Constable asked if he'd like to check his phone messages first, which made me raise my head.

The guy said no, and that he normally ignores 'the shit the missus sends us'. The sergeant asked again, 'Are you sure?' The guy eventually took the phone back.

Turned out his girlfriend had warned him by text that there were police parked near their flat pulling over suspected drunk drivers.

Sergeant, Thirsk

Big Brother

I was going back through old CCTV footage whilst working on a case when I saw a bizarre incident unfolding at the house next door.

A very drunk young woman staggered up to the door at about 4am with a large brick in hand, intent on causing some damage. She hurled the brick at the door, only to discover that the window was made of safety glass. The brick rebounded straight into her face. She staggered off clutching her face with blood dripping through her fingers.

Detective Inspector, Sheffield

Deep, Dark Secrets

In our station, I and my colleagues have found, amongst many others things, the following during full-body searches: a flick-knife inside a vagina, stolen computer chips in a man's cheek, a diamond ring up someone's nose, two ecstasy tablets in a particularly accommodating foreskin, an ounce of cannabis behind a prosthetic nipple and a dog biscuit under a very large man's moob.

One tip from the professionals. Don't hide things in your rectum. It's the first place we look.

Constable, Manchester

What's in a Name?

I was part of a team searching a block of flats for Class-A drugs. We knew someone in the area was dealing, but nobody was talking. After one doorstep interview we asked to take the guy's details just in case we needed to get back in touch.

He couldn't remember his phone number, so he asked one of his posse to get the number from his phone. Once he found the number, he passed the phone over to me so I could take it down. The name was listed as 'Dealer Dave'. We immediately called in the sniffer dogs and they found a sizable stash under the floorboards.

Detective Sergeant, Bristol

Horse Sense

A mate was part of the mounted branch
and had been on a three hour patrol with
a colleague. They were just about to call
it a day when a man, not looking where he
was going, walked right into the side of
his horse.

Instead of apologising, he swore loudly
and punched the horse in the neck. Failing
to look where he was going cost him £350.

Constable, London

Mistaken Identity

A young woman, with long blonde hair, called us to report that a rather creepy customer was waiting for her outside the bar where she worked. We take these calls seriously, and an officer was dispatched to ensure she wasn't menaced or worse.

When he arrived the girl apologised because the man had finally left. The officer was about to depart when the girl's phone rang. It was a fellow barman who also had long hair who'd just been followed down the street as he left work and had his arse felt. The perpetrator was just as shocked to see a bloke turning around as he was to receive a punch in the face.

Chief Inspector, Coventry

Talking Dirty

Emergency operators were at the end of their tethers with nuisance caller who insisted on phoning a few times each week to talk dirty.

This happened about fifteen times in the course of a month and we were asked to take action. He was easy to trace. When I arrived to arrest him, all he could say was, 'Shit, not again!'

Sergeant, Bolton

Power Nap

Late on a weeknight I found a van parked on the side of a country road. The guy in the driver's seat was very drunk and had passed out over the passenger seat and had his legs sticking out of the driver's window. He was oblivious to my arrival despite the blue flashing lights. I had to shake him awake.

When he finally came to, he looked at me for a second, straightened up in the seat, fixed his clothes a bit, put on his seat belt, leaned out the window, then said, 'Is there a problem, offisher?'

Constable, Salisbury

Knife to Meet You

We were called out to a burglary during the night, and arrived to find the home-owners out on the street waiting for us. The lady of the house had the forethought to pull on her dressing gown, but her man had only thought to grab a knife on his way out the door.

There is no sight more disconcerting than a balding middle-aged man in Y-fronts, wielding an offensive 12 inch blade.

WPC, Milton Keynes

Outstanding in His Field

I ended up in a scuffle with a few pissed-up farmers who'd got a bit rowdy at the NFU club in town. We scrapped for a while, before one of them got me on the ground in the middle of the road. The guy was huge, absolutely dwarfing me, so it was hardly a fair fight.

Suddenly I heard someone scream 'CAR!' and the screech of tyres on tarmac. The guy I was grappling with somehow managed to drag us both out of the way just as my discarded hat disappeared beneath the wheels. The farmers were in such shock they gave themselves up immediately, thankful that they were only being charged with assaulting a police officer rather than being murderous cop killers.

Constable, Hereford

A Date With Destiny

A teenager made off with a bottle of rum from the supermarket where I work.

When I returned to the store, having failed to catch him down the street, a girl approached me holding out her phone. He had chatted her up in the fruit and veg aisle and had given her his phone number. It didn't take long to track him down.

Store Detective, Leeds

Plumbing the Depths

A legendary case from the Glasgow Sheriff Court was this man being tried for theft. The less than on-the-ball Fiscal, checking his notes, asked the defendant, 'Mr McGlinchy, by your own admission you were caught stealing taps. Are you a plumber?'

'Naw, sir.'

'Do you know a plumber, Mr McGlinchy?'

'Naw, sir.'

'Do you have contacts in the building trade?'

'Naw.'

'How then were you planning to dispose of your loot?'

'Easy, like… they were Celtic taps.'

Advocate, Glasgow

Bad Parole Model

I was once called out to a fight at a local tennis club. When I arrived both men in question were at either sides of the court nursing their wounds.

They'd got into a fight over a disputed point and one smacked the other over the back of the head with his racquet. Then all hell had broken loose.

Once they'd calmed down and been warned about their behaviour, I made them shake hands and, to lighten the mood, asked who had been winning. One replied immediately, 'Oh, we weren't playing a proper match, we were just having a knockabout to warm up.'

Constable, Cambridge

Only a Game

One of my clients was due in for a drugs test as part of the conditions of his early release, but arrived about two hours late.

Suspicious, I took a urine sample and sent it for testing. He was flabbergasted to discover he'd tested positive for cannabis, convinced it would've left his system after three days.

He'd deliberately delayed his test by two hours to reach the necessary 72 hour window. He didn't realise that this is only the case if you haven't been smoking hash most days since you were fifteen.

Probation Officer, London

Anti-Social Work

I was on my way out to see a new client
- a man in his early forties who'd been
released from a short term sentence and
was experiencing serious withdrawal since
he'd given up drink and drugs. I was
keen to make a good first impression
- in social work, first impressions count
for a lot. I'd planned out the visit in my
head before I even got in the car.

When I arrived, I greeted him with a
smile, and the conversation began to flow
comfortably. Until I accidentally trod
on his pet hamster and broke its neck.
Needless to say, I was reassigned.

Social Worker, Newcastle-upon-Tyne

Loaded Weapon

A naked man was brandishing a firearm in the street. We were closest when the call came in and were first on the scene.

It was our job to secure the area and keep the public a safe distance in an attempt to prevent fatalities while an armed response unit was scrambled. This kind of scenario is always high stress. One wrong move and someone can lose their life. When we arrived I was relieved to see that the guy was clearly holding a water pistol rather than a real gun, and was either very drunk or high. Just as well because he could've been shot.

What was most memorable though was that he had the biggest penis I have ever seen and, to make matters worse, was brandishing a huge erection. The effect of whatever he'd consumed or the excitement of the situation, who knows?

Sergeant, Aberdeen

Tattoo Artist

I remember a man I was defending being tried in court for armed robbery. The prosecution counsel seemed very glum, not his usual ebullient self, which I took as the result of a distinct lack of evidence. I was confident my client hadn't committed the crime and hoped to gain an acquittal.

On the third day of the trial, however, my opposite number was back with his normal bounce, and asked to resume questioning immediately. When he requested the accused roll his trouser leg up, I was about to intervene, but noticed a tattoo on his calf.

It turned out the guy had been tattooing the dates and locations of each of his robberies onto his leg. All the Police had to do was match them with reported crimes. It was an uphill task after that to keep him out of jail.

Barrister, Liverpool

Women's Things

A WPC colleague and I were called to a disturbance - students were having a party in their living room that had continued well into the night and the neighbours weren't happy. It was pretty clear from the astronaut that answered the door that illegal substances were being taken, so we started telling people to turn out their pockets and empty their bags.

I was searching one girl's handbag which included a box of tampons that, without really thinking, I put back without examining.

My female colleague saw what I'd done and immediately took the box and removed the contents, finding hash, MDMA and cocaine. That'll teach me to be gallant.

Constable, London

Location, Location, Location

I was sitting in my office ploughing through some paperwork when the pungent smell of weed drifted through my open window. I stuck my head out and directly below three young lads had wandered down a back street for a cheeky toke, not realising they were leaning against the back wall of the station.

I sent an officer down to put the frighteners on them, caution them and send them on their way.

Detective Chief Inspector, Swansea

Use the Force

I pulled over a couple of guys for speeding last year, but I had to let them off with a warning when the driver rolled down the window and said 'These are not the droids you're looking for', gently waving his hand in front of my face.

He's lucky he was pulled over by a fellow Star Wars fan or he'd have been fined and breathalysed.

Constable, Brighton

Urine Trouble

A drug user on probation tried to fool me during a urine test with a homemade apparatus filled with a friend's wee.

The sleight of hand didn't work though, and he ended up spilling half of it down himself. The irony was his friend's sample tested positive too.

Probation Officer, Nottingham

Smoke and Mirrors

We were sent to a reported incident which involved searching for an alleged gunman.

I was convinced that I'd spotted him through a house window and immediately raised my weapon and held him in my sights. He was armed and responded instantly by pointing his gun at me too.

After a stand-off of a couple of minutes, as I yelled into my radio for backup, I lowered my gun, made a couple of hand waves, and realised I'd been confronting myself in a mirror.

Tactical Firearms Officer, London

The Law is Mightier Than The Sword

I once had to arrest a bloke on Halloween who was carrying a full-on Samurai sword down the street. He looked at me in shock, saying, 'But it's Halloween!'

Constable, Belfast

On Your Bike, Son

It's pretty funny watching someone trying
to ride a bike when they're drunk, but
it's less funny when they veer into
oncoming traffic.

The number of times I've had to pull
over drunk cyclists and insist that they
walk their bike home. One guy decided he'd
try and outrun me. I was on foot, called
for him to stop but he sped off, wobbled,
hit a kerb and went straight over the
handlebars, landing face first in some dog
crap. It's called Karma, I believe.

Constable, Cardiff

Say My Name

Several buses had been heavily vandalised while parked in the bus depot, causing thousands of pounds worth of damage.

The youths were visible on CCTV, but too distant to be recognisable. We'd probably never have caught them if one hadn't felt the urge to scrawl his own name in spray paint across one of the windscreens.

Detective Sergeant, Glasgow

Put It Away

I felt very much the knight in shining armour one night when I thought I'd stumbled upon a sexual assault in the local park.

I realised my mistake when both parties told me to 'fuck off', hastily covering themselves with discarded items of clothing. They still received a warning about their behaviour.

Police Community Support Officer, Chesterfield

Window Pain

I was called to meet a social worker who was concerned because one of her clients wasn't answering the door, though she could hear him banging around inside the flat. I was trying to squint through the window when a fist came flying through the glass, hitting me square on the nose.

Remarkably I didn't get any shards of glass in my eyes. I shouldered the door of the flat, preparing to defend myself, but was met by an idiot who had only just realised that punching someone through a window would split his hand open in a dozen places.

He was crying like a baby as blood dripped all over his hall carpet. This made it much easier to arrest him.

Sergeant, Birmingham

Feline Nine Nine

A distraught woman called us late one Sunday night to report a murder.

As I took the call, the adrenalin surged through me. I knew this could be big. Although she was pretty garbled, she managed to explain that she and her partner had got drunk and had a huge fight. One thing led to another, and the bloke, in a blind rage, threw her cat out of their second-story window.

When the Police arrived he'd fled the scene and, of course, the cat was sitting in the front garden none the worse for its defenestration.

Emergency Call Handler, Manchester

Heroin Chic

We received a tip-off from a well-known photography chain. An amateur snapper had decided to take some very arty photos at a party in his flat, and happened to be one of the last people left in the world still using roll film.

There were quite a few shots of people snorting and injecting various substances, but this hadn't deterred the wannabe David Bailey. Helpfully he had provided the photo processors with his full address so we paid him a visit and found large quantities of Class A drugs at his home.

Detective Sergeant, London

What He Would Have Wanted

Two officers from our station were called out by the neighbour of a middle-aged man who hadn't been seen leaving or entering his home in over two weeks. He had health problems so she was concerned.

When they broke down the front door the stench was overpowering and they found him dead in his armchair. The guy had had two cats and, when they hadn't been fed in a few days, they'd chewed the flesh off of his legs and feet, pretty much down to the bone.

After the body was removed the RSPCA was called but, by all accounts, the moggies were none the worse for their 'ordeal'.

Constable, Dover

Tit For Tat

We once pulled a girl over on the motorway for driving erratically, suspecting she was under the influence.

By the time I got to the car window she had managed to strip off her shirt and her bra, and innocently asked 'What's the problem, officer?' My female colleague wasn't impressed to say the least. To make matters worse, when breathalysed, the driver was stone cold sober.

Constable, British Transport Police

Search Inside Yourself

I ended up in a very uncomfortable situation when my sniffer dog, Alfie, singled out a man in the queue for security at Heathrow airport.

We took the guy into a private room and searched his hand-luggage, clothing and footwear, turning up around two kilos of cocaine. Alfie was still convinced that the guy had something on him, but we had thoroughly strip-searched him, and examined his clothing and shoes. All that was left to do was a cavity search.

After a few minutes, with my index finger thrust up his bum, he eventually blurted out that he had a concealed pocket in his jacket, and that there was a small pouch of cocaine hidden there – that's what Alfie could smell. He'd already been caught. I don't know why he didn't admit to it earlier.

Border Force Officer, London

What Were Ewe Thinking?

We received a call from an elderly couple who had been rambling in the Scottish countryside when they heard a man's voice encouraging someone to engage in sexual relations with him.

Curious, they followed the voice and, over a hillock, found a fully naked man in his late 50's, demanding that a sheep "have a go" of his dick. When we eventually arrived, he was long gone, and I wondered whether it'd be some kind of shared hallucination between the pensioners. However later that day we spotted a cocky-looking bloke who matched their description striding down the road, stripped to the waist in what could only be described as bracing weather.

Without any real evidence, all we could do was stop and warn the weirdo that we'd be keeping an eye on him.

Constable, Inverness

Dangerous Eruption

A woman called to report a suspicious looking man who had just wandered slowly down her quiet street, looking into the window of several cars as he passed. She was certain he was going to break into one when he spotted something tasty.

I was in a patrol car and managed to locate the guy a few streets away, and observed him doing the same, stopping every few vehicles and peering into the windows, no attempt to hide what he was doing. I approached and challenged him to explain what he was up to. He looked totally embarrassed, saying that he was meeting a girl and that he had just burst a spot on his chin that wouldn't stop bleeding. He didn't want to turn up to a date with blood all over his face, and he was trying to check his reflection in the car windows. I shone my flashlight on him and sure enough the zit was a belter. A real Krakatoa.

WPC, Scunthorpe

Lifted

I was called out to assist with two young men who had caused some trouble in Waverley Station in Edinburgh. They thought it would be funny to kick the doors of a lift until it jammed.

Bizarrely they decided to do this from the inside, which of course meant they were trapped. I made sure the engineer didn't rush.

Constable, British Transport Police

Hiss-terical

In the mid-90s I was on my way with a colleague to arrest a suspected dealer. We banged on the door a couple of times, but there was no reply. Then we heard someone opening an upstairs window. Before we knew it, large writhing creatures began to drop onto our heads. Snakes!

We fell over each other to get out of the way, and had to wait for animal control to arrive before we could safely apprehend the suspect. I'm well over six feet tall and it took all my self-control to not scream like a girl. Not the most noble moment of my career…

Detective Inspector, Ipswich

Till Death Do Us Fart

Think on this story the next time you contemplate breaking wind in front of your partner. We were alerted by some neighbours who could hear ferocious screaming coming from one of the houses on their street.

After her husband let rip with a massive fart right in her face, a woman had gone berserk and thrown several kitchen knives at his head. Luckily her aim was terrible.

Sergeant, Derby

You Total Tube

If you don't want to get caught, it's best to avoid having an entire YouTube channel dedicated to your criminal enterprises.

They don't call it the information superhighway for nothing.

Detective Inspector, Sheffield

Plane Embarrassing

There was a fracas underway at a discount airline check-in desk - not uncommon - so I thought I'd offer to help calm the situation. A woman was swearing at the assistant, kicking the desk and waving her phone around.

When I asked the problem, she shouted 'I have my boarding pass on my phone! Why can't she just scan it?' (The idiot had taken a photo of a printed pass rather than used the airline's app). She thrust her phone under my nose, and in doing so skipped to the previous photo which, to my visible horror, showed her and her partner involved in graphic coitus that would make a porn star blush. My eyes popped out on stalks and I flushed with embarrassment.

Seeing my reaction, she burst out into shameless laughter. At least it diffused the tension and calmed her down.

Security Officer, Gatwick Airport

What Goes Around

I had to pull over one day to intervene in a fight that had broken out in the middle of the street.

I had just managed to force the two guys apart when one of them booted me hard between the legs. I went down like a ton of bricks, tears in my eyes, head swimming. The guy concerned legged it, jumping a high wall into a garden.

However, instead of hearing the thump of him landing, I heard a scream of pain. I got to my feet, hobbled across the road and peered over the wall. In his haste he had landed on a large metal pole that had penetrated right into his groin.

Constable, Hull

Fool Moon

I was driving with my partner, having a fairly uneventful night. We were griping about how bored we were when into our headlights appeared a man's naked arse, protruding from some bushes.

When we stopped the car to investigate, a woman's shocked face appeared beside it, and then both face and bum disappeared into the undergrowth sharpish.

We couldn't give chase because we were laughing too much.

Constable, Reigate

Dirty Protest

When I was in training, I pulled over an executive type in a high-performance car for speeding. It was my first stop and I was experiencing some nerves.

As I approached, the guy lowered his window. He had a wild look in his eyes and seemed very upset. When I asked if he knew why I'd stopped him, he said, "Of course, I was speeding... But I need to get home now! I have a bowel complaint and I'm about to shit myself! My house is just round the corner..." At that moment he let out a huge groan and horrible watery fart. One sniff confirmed his worst fears had been realised.

The poor guy was totally mortified so I let him on his way, feeling rather guilty that he might have made it if I hadn't stopped him.

Constable, British Transport Police

Pulling the Emergency Handle

I was representing a train driver at a tribunal after a piece of workplace misconduct. Some passengers were getting irate at the delay to their service and, after fifteen minutes, having had no announcement from the driver, demanded the conductor find out what was taking so long.

When he got to the driver's cabin at the front of the train, he had to immediately withdraw as the driver had his trousers round his knees.

While he'd been waiting for an emergency stop signal to change he'd got bored and decided to crack one off. Literally caught with his trousers down.

Solicitor, Southampton

An Open and Shut Case

One night, we were told to go to a semi where neighbours had heard violent banging through the adjoining wall.

Having receiving no answer when we knocked, but hearing a violent commotion through the letterbox, we feared the worst and broke down the door. A terrible racket was coming from the first floor. We raced up the stairs and burst into a bedroom to find a wardrobe rocking backwards and forwards against the wall.

For a moment I thought I was witnessing poltergeist activity but then a voice called out for help. When we opened the wardrobe a man and a woman emerged, he was stark bollock naked and she was dressed as Zorro.

Sergeant, Paisley

Winter Blunderland

We were called to investigate a robbery that had occurred a couple of days after what had turned out to be a very white Christmas. Lots of people go away to visit relatives between Chrtistmas and New Year, making it the ideal time for an enterprising housebreaker.

Having checked out the property, I noticed a visible set of footprints leading away from the backdoor, which had been forced open.

Not expecting them to go anywhere useful, we decided to follow them anyway. They led us into the back garden of the house next door where we found the thief emerging from a broken ground floor window.

Sergeant, Bristol

UniformDating.com

Halloween is always one of the busiest nights of the year for us – fights break out all over the place and everyone is off their face on drugs and/or booze.

As we patrolled the Promenade, an inebriated young woman dressed as Snow White took a fancy to my uniform and came over to tell me so, putting an arm around my neck and kissing me on the cheek.

Her boyfriend, in full Batman outfit, was getting steamed up about it, and came over looking for a fight, balling his fists and puffing out his chest, squaring up to me. Before he could embarrass himself I took out my ID, demonstrating that I was in fact not wearing a costume.

Constable, Blackpool

Engine Trouble

Here's a tip based on my own experience - if you need to take your car to the garage, remember to remove the drugs you stashed in the glove compartment and under the front seat.

And don't forget about the coke in the boot. The mechanic may not always be happy about it.

Detective Sergeant, London

Hardware and Software

I once arrested a guy who had been stealing mobile phones. What we didn't realise until we caught him was that he had been sending photos of his erect and flaccid penis to random phone contacts he'd found on each.

When I asked him why he'd done it, all he could say was, 'Why not?' Hard to argue with that logic.

Constable, Norwich

Stung

I pride myself on being quite physically
fit, so chasing offenders isn't a problem
for me.

Apart from one time, a few years ago,
when I was led on a chase into some
woods. I managed to catch up with the guy,
brought him down and got the cuffs on him.
But then I felt prickly pain in my ankles.

Thinking I'd landed in a nettle patch,
I looked down. As the buzzing got louder,
we both realised what was happening. The
bees chased us all the way back to the
patrol car.

Constable, Dundee

Money Shot

I remember being called out by some people who had been terrified by gunshots coming from a property above them. When we arrived, there was silence at the flat and nobody seemed to be around.

All we could see was a large puddle of blood, which turned our stomachs. We called around the local hospitals looking for the guy who lived at the flat, and found him within a couple of minutes.

When we arrived, we immediately interviewed him. Two important pieces of information emerged. Firstly, he'd shot himself in the testicles with a shotgun, and two, he didn't have a permit to own the weapon.

It felt pretty rough arresting a bloke who's just shot himself in the balls.

Sergeant, Ripon

Dungeon by the Hour

I picked up a guy staggering along the road, drunk as a skunk and dressed in a gimp costume. He was largely unresponsive, and clearly in no state to get home by himself, so I decided to put him in a cell for the night.

When we arrived back at the station he perked up, and asked if I'd be putting him in handcuffs. I told him that as long as he remained docile then it wouldn't be necessary, to which he replied that, in fact, he'd be very, very naughty.

We locked him up, to his obvious delight. I remember the Duty Sergeant muttering that we should really be charging him by the hour.

Constable, Guildford

Gentleman's Rules

We arrested a posh nutter for committing grievous bodily harm with a cricket bat to his next door neighbour. It turned out that the victim had borrowed the suspect's lawnmower several months previously and had failed to give it back, despite numerous requests.

As we led the cricketer away he shouted over his shoulder at his neighbour who was being loaded into an ambulance, "Good job it was a cricket bat. My other sport's shooting!" Since he was the holder of a valid firearms license we took that as a Threat to Kill under the Offences Against the Person Act 1861 section 16. The judge saw it the same way.

Sergeant, Sevenoaks

Golden Shower

After fifteen years in what is now the Border Force nothing has beaten the time I stopped someone arriving from the sub-continent. There was nothing outwardly suspicious about the man – he was moving normally – but as I was checking his luggage he became more and more insistent that he had to leave.

We were concerned he may be a drug mule, so I performed a cavity search. During the examination, I encountered a hard, rectangular object in the man's rectum. This I removed, and was astonished to find out how heavy it was – a gold ingot, weighting an ounce (according to the stamp on it).

In total I removed twelve ingots, which had a value of twelve thousand pounds sterling at the time. Apparently there is a 10% tax on exported gold from India which the guy was trying to avoid.

Border Force Officer, London

Fish Supper

A couple of teenagers went into a petshop, one carrying a pint glass full of water, and asked to buy a goldfish.

The owner of the shop fished one out, but as she was about to put it in the standard plastic bag the boys asked her to put it in the glass instead, saying that they lived across the road and it'd be easier.

When the goldfish was deposited into the pint glass the one holding it raised the glass, shouted, 'Down the hatch!', and drank water, fish and all as the other filmed it on his iPhone. Then they ran out of the shop laughing. It was when they posted the video on Facebook that we got them for cruelty to animals.

Constable, Croydon

Art of War

I took a statement from a 71-year-old pensioner who, despite being zapped six times by a Taser, fought off a would-be thief trying to gain entry to his home.

The crook knocked on the man's door and asked if he had a leak. When the septuagenarian told him he didn't, the thug threw a number of punches trying to force entry. The 71-year-old dodged the first punch and began throwing haymakers of his own.

Realising he had bitten off more than he could chew, the robber pulled out a stun gun and shocked the man six times in the neck. This did not deter the pensioner who continued to hammer down blows and ultimately the thief ran off. The victim was taken to hospital as a precaution but released soon after.

Constable, London

Peep Show

We arrested a man for public indecency after he stuck his penis through a hole in a pub cubicle wall, hoping for a 'wet present' from whoever was sitting on the adjacent toilet.

Unfortunately for him the hole was rather tight. The man's penis became trapped. His frantic efforts to remove his member only made it swell, jamming it further.

When soap and olive oil didn't work, the Fire Service had to use cutting equipment to free him.

Sergeant, Kendal

Dangerous Weapon

We were responding to a domestic taking place on the upper walkway of a block of flats. The woman had thrown her belongings into some bin bags, hoping to get away before her partner got home, but had been caught in the act.

When we arrived they were going at it tooth and claw; who did what to whom, when and how many times, etc. Despite our best efforts to calm things down they were completely focused on yelling at each other. At one point the male grabbed for one of the bags and tore it open, spilling the contents.

He stopped and shouted, 'What the hell is that?!' She grabbed the item in question and, brandishing it, said, 'That's my dildo, coz you don't satisfy me!' She continued bawling at him, waving the shlong in his face, until we had to restrain her from beating him with it.

Constable, Liverpool

Stunted

It has to have been the worst escape attempt I have ever seen; we trapped a car thief on a bridge near the M1.

He jumped out of the stolen vehicle and ran to the edge of the bridge. Seeing a lorry approaching he decided to channel some 007 magic and attempted to leap onto the back of it.

He almost pulled it off but, failing to appreciate the backdraft, landed face first onto the artic's trailer. He broke all his teeth, fractured his jaw and skull and required his tongue to be stitched back into his mouth after he bit most of it off.

There didn't seem much point in reminding him of his 'right to remain silent' but we did so anyway. Incredible that he wasn't killed.

Sergeant, Stevenage

Pinned to Rights

A guy decided to rob a petrol station with a crossbow. He barged in brandishing the weapon, demanding cash.

As the assistant hand over the contents of the till, in his excitement the thief shot himself in the foot with the bolt, pinning it to the floor. Not too hard to catch after that.

WPC, Stoke-on-Trent

Piece of Piss

We were called to a precinct following the mugging of a pensioner. As I took a statement, I asked her if she'd had a lot of valuables in the bag that the thief had taken.

The woman seemed none the worse for her ordeal and in fact quite chipper considering what she'd been through. She said, 'Don't worry dear, when that young man has a look inside he'll realise that all I keep in there these days is my colostomy bag.'

Constable, Newcastle-upon-Tyne

Criminal Behaviour